you shall above all things be glad and young.
For if you're young,whatever life you wear

it will become you;and if you are glad
whatever's living will yourself become.
Girlboys may nothing more than boygirls need:
I can entirely her only love

whose any mystery makes every man's

flesh put space on;and his mind take off time

that you should ever think,may god forbid
and(in his mercy)your true lover spare:
for that way knowledge lies,the foetal grave
called progress,and negation's dead undoom.

I'd rather learn from one bird how to sing
than teach ten thousand stars how not to dance

From *Collected Poems*

VOICES · IN · POETRY

E. E. CUMMINGS   S. L. BERRY

ARTWORK BY STASYS EIDRIGEVICIUS

CREATIVE ❦ EDUCATION

Ezra Pound once encouraged his fellow poets to "make it new." Edward Estlin Cummings (1894–1962), or e. e. cummings (self-named in his poems), took that dictum to another planet, farther than any other English or American poet.

Even as a child, Cummings knew what he wanted to be. From the ages of 8 to 22, he wrote a poem a day. By the time he graduated from Harvard, his avant-garde forms and eccentric syntax spilled letters of words down the page, and he juggled verbs, adverbs, and adjectives as if they were nouns, gleefully violating grammar's rules. He reveled in new word combinations such as "balloonman," "mud-luscious," and "eddieandbill." Yet for all that, and despite being influenced by Pound and Gertrude Stein, many of Cummings's poems are quite traditional and in sonnet form.

No matter how peculiar, jarring, or even incomprehensible Cummings's poems appeared in print—with letters jammed together to encourage speed reading or split apart to tell the reader where to pause—the abiding theme of this "intelligent experimenter," as one reviewer called him, remained constant. That theme was love, especially for his father, who died in 1926, and of whom the younger Cummings wrote, "my father moved through dooms of love."

Cummings opposed progress, that "comfortable disease," the arrogance of science and technology, which he saw as the antithesis of nature. "Listen," he wrote in "Pity this busy monster, manukind," "there's a hell / of a good universe next door; let's go."

After 1930, Cummings's emotional devices and "old-fashioned poetry," as some called it, fell out of favor. Others still see his greatest failure as being flagrant sentimentalism. For a time, his star was eclipsed by the more intellectual modern poets. But the candor and freshness of his form—his lyricism is unmistakable—indisputably rank him as one of America's most inventive poets, endlessly trying new ways, as he put it, to "paint a picture."

– *J. Patrick Lewis, United States Children's Poet Laureate (2011-13)*

"If a poet is anybody, he is somebody to whom things made matter very little—somebody who is obsessed by Making."

E. E. Cummings made this observation in the introduction to *is Five*. He was, himself, a poet obsessed by Making. Combining an artist's sense of visual composition with a writer's sense of verbal manipulation, he created poems that looked and sounded entirely new.

Cummings was an odd combination of avant-garde modernist and old-fashioned lyricist. A staunch believer in the rights of the individual, he wrote biting, satirical poems that were critical of the dehumanizing aspects of industry and government. Yet he was also an unabashed romantic, writing lovely, lyrical poems that celebrated nature and the human spirit. And despite their disjointed appearance, many of his poems were written in traditional rhymed and metered verse forms.

Foregoing commercial success for artistic experimentation, Cummings created poems so unique that they permanently altered poetry's artistic boundaries. In the process, he earned a reputation as one of America's most daring and innovative poets.

E. E. Cummings, poet and artist

l(a

le
af
fa

ll

s)
one
l

iness

From *95 Poems*

7

Edward Estlin Cummings was born on October 14, 1894, in Cambridge, Massachusetts, the first of two children born to Edward and Rebecca Cummings. Estlin's sister, Elizabeth, was born in 1896.

Edward Cummings Sr. was the first professor of sociology at Harvard University; he later became the minister of one of Boston's most respected Unitarian churches. He was an excellent writer and speaker, inciting in Estlin a fascination with language and word play. He was also a skilled carpenter and taught his son to use his hands as well as his mind.

Rebecca Cummings was a warm, happy woman who loved spending time with her children. She sang to them and played games with them. She also taught both of them to read. An avid diary-keeper and amateur poet, Rebecca introduced Estlin to the pleasure of writing while he was still quite young, recording his diary entries for him, then urging him to add illustrations.

Estlin grew up in a spacious, sunny house that his father told him he had built "in order to have you in." His neighborhood was full of children, most of them the offspring of Harvard professors. Estlin and his friends roamed the nearby woods, playing cops and robbers or blind man's bluff. In the winter, they skated on a local pond; in the summer, they played baseball on vacant lots. And regardless of the season, when they wanted to rest, they retreated to Estlin's treehouse, a roomy, sturdy place with a porch and small working stove on which they toasted apples and popped corn.

Each summer, the Cummings family spent several weeks at Joy Farm, their rural residence near Silver Lake, New Hampshire. Estlin spent his days there exploring woods and pastures while learning how to use a compass and to identify wildlife. His evenings were spent with books—a family tradition was to have one member read aloud every evening.

As an adult, Cummings acknowledged the tremendous impact his parents had had on him, stating that it had been "my joyous fate and my supreme good fortune" to belong to such a family.

Edward Cummings Sr., with Estlin and Elizabeth

CHANSONS INNOCENTES: I

in Just-
spring   when the world is mud-
luscious the little
lame balloonman

whistles   far   and wee

and eddieandbill come
running from marbles and
piracies and it's
spring

when the world is puddle-wonderful

the queer
old balloonman whistles
far   and wee
and bettyandisbel come dancing

from hop-scotch and jump-rope and

it's
spring
and
   the

      goat-footed

balloonMan   whistles
far
and
wee

From Tulips and Chimneys

EDUCATION

Because learning and literature were so valued in his family, Estlin grew up surrounded by books. Among his favorites were *The Arabian Nights*, *The Odyssey*, and *King Arthur and His Knights*. His family's evening readings also introduced him to Charles Dickens's *David Copperfield* and Robert Louis Stevenson's *Treasure Island*.

At the age of eight, Estlin began attending private school. When he transferred to a nearby public school two years later, his reading skills were so advanced that he was promoted to the seventh grade. He was only 12 years old when he enrolled as a freshman in the Cambridge Latin School, a college preparatory program housed in a building next to Cambridge High School.

Estlin was a good student, though not outstanding. As required, he studied Latin, French, and Greek, besides reading books from Harvard's recommended reading list. He also wrote for the school's monthly *Cambridge Review*, eventually serving as its literary editor in his senior year. But neither his own writing nor the words he selected for the *Review* hinted at the literary maverick Estlin would become.

Cambridge Latin School, which was demolished in 1980

all ignorance toboggans into know
and trudges up to ignorance again:
but winter's not forever,even snow
melts;and if spring should spoil the game,
    what then?

all history's a winter sport or three:
but were it five,i'd still insist that all
history is too small for even me;
for me and you,exceedingly too small.

Swoop(shrill collective myth)into thy grave
merely to toil the scale to shrillerness
per every madge and mabel dick and dave
—tomorrow is our permanent address

and there they'll scarcely find us(if they do,
we'll move away still further:into now

From *1 x 1*

13

COLLEGE

In 1911, Estlin graduated from the Latin School and headed down the street to Harvard University. Academically, Estlin spent his time deepening his understanding of languages. He concentrated on Greek studies, but he also took courses in Spanish and German. He broadened his literary background by studying Shakespeare and lyric poetry.

As important as his academic courses were to him, Estlin's leisure-time activities were even more so. He loved circuses and ballets, operas and ragtime piano bars, amusement parks and symphonies. He also loved the company of young women. Pale and blond with hazel eyes and high cheekbones, Estlin had good looks, a quick smile, and an enthusiasm for life that attracted women to him. He was an excellent dancer and an incorrigible romantic. On more than one Sunday morning, his mother had to hurriedly clean the hairpins out of the back seat of the family car before her husband drove it to church.

As his social life got livelier, Estlin's artistic interest expanded. He fell in with a group of freethinkers and became acquainted with the Cubists' experiments in painting. A self-taught painter in both oil and watercolor, Estlin began to try his hand at abstracts. His interest in Cubism soon spilled over into his creative writing, and it was during this time that Estlin first began rearranging sentences and spacing words on a page in an attempt to achieve specific visual and verbal effects.

His new pursuits put Estlin in conflict with his more conservative father, who couldn't understand his son's desire for personal and artistic experimentation. Refusing to recognize Estlin as an adult, Edward Sr. often treated him as a stubborn, wayward child. The result was a frustrating series of arguments and shouting matches.

By the time Estlin graduated from Harvard in 1916, he was ready to leave Cambridge for good.

SONNETS—REALITIES: I

the Cambridge ladies who live in furnished souls
are unbeautiful and have comfortable minds
(also, with the church's protestant blessings
daughters, unscented shapeless spirited)
they believe in Christ and Longfellow, both dead,
are invariably interested in so many things—
at the present writing one still finds
delighted fingers knitting for the is it Poles?
perhaps. While permanent faces coyly bandy
scandal of Mrs. N and Professor D
.... the Cambridge ladies do not care, above
Cambridge if sometimes in its box of
sky lavender and cornerless, the
moon rattles like a fragment of angry candy

From Tulips and Chimneys

In January of 1917, Cummings moved to Greenwich Village, New York City, where he'd landed a job at a publishing company. Bored with his daily routine, however, he soon quit. He planned to live life on his own terms, he told his parents, as a painter and a poet.

But the world interfered with his plans. On April 6, 1917, the United States officially entered World War I. Faced with the likelihood of being drafted, Cummings enlisted as a driver in the Norton-Harjes Ambulance Corps. Though a pacifist, Cummings had no desire to go to prison for his beliefs; ambulance service seemed the least objectionable way to take part in a war he didn't believe in. Ironically, he ended up in prison anyway.

Cummings and Slater Brown, a friend from Harvard who also had enlisted in the ambulance service, were sent to France. When they reached their unit in the French countryside, their disdain for military discipline and for following orders led to their arrests as suspected German spies. They were imprisoned in a former seminary in a small French village, along with 40 other men from various countries.

The prisoners spent their days in one large room where they slept, talked, read, and otherwise tried to cope with boredom and fear. The poor diet and lack of hygiene took its toll as well, and illnesses were common. Already slender, Cummings became rail thin; a vitamin deficiency led to a skin rash and depression.

After three months, Cummings was released, thanks to contacts his father had in Washington. (Brown was released a short while later.) Though it was a miserable ordeal, Cummings's imprisonment did serve a purpose: It became the subject of his first book, *The Enormous Room*, a prose account of his experiences published in 1922.

World War I doughboys

I lift my eyes. I am standing in a tiny oblong space. A sort of court. All around, two-story wooden barracks. Little crude staircases lead up to doors heavily chained and immensely padlocked. More like ladders than stairs. Curious hewn windows, smaller in proportion than the slits in a doll's house. Are these faces behind the slits? The doors bulge incessantly under the shock of bodies hurled against them from within. The whole dirty *nouveau* business about to crumble.

Glance one.

Glance two: directly before me. A wall with many bars fixed across one minute opening. At the opening a dozen, fifteen, grins. Upon the bars hands, scraggy and bluishly white. Through the bars stretching of lean arms, incessant stretchings. The grins leap at the window, hands belonging to them catch hold, arms belonging to the hands stretch in my direction … an instant; then new grins leap from behind and knock off the first grins which go down with a fragile crashing like glass smashed: hands wither and break, arms streak out of sight, sucked inward.

From *The Enormous Room*

Despite his efforts to avoid active duty, Cummings was drafted in May 1918. But by the time his basic training ended, so had the war. He then spent six months at an army camp in Massachusetts, chafing at the restrictiveness of military life.

Military service was not a positive experience, but it did give Cummings time to think. By the time he returned to New York City in 1919, he had formulated a basic set of values that shaped the way he lived for the rest of his life. The 24-year-old had concluded that, as an artist and a poet, he valued the acts of painting and writing more than the resulting pictures and poems. On a social level, he preferred the company of nonconformists and people who were uncorrupted by privilege and power. And personally, he balked at any attempt to restrict his freedom to think, say, and do as he pleased; he had no intention of conforming to anyone else's idea of acceptable standards.

Many of these values were reflected in Cummings's writing. For example, the most famous of his stylistic devices—his use of the lowercase "i" as a personal pronoun—came about as a result of his admiration for the handyman who took care of the Cummings family cottage on Silver Lake, near Joy Farm. Poorly educated, he wrote letters to Cummings's father in which he referred to himself as "i"; the humbleness this suggested was very appealing to Cummings.

i sing of Olaf glad and big
whose warmest heart recoiled at war:
a conscientious object-or

his wellbeloved colonel(trig
westpointer most succinctly bred)
took erring Olaf soon in hand;
but—though an host of overjoyed
noncoms(first knocking on the head
him)do through icy waters roll
that helplessness which others stroke
with brushes recently employed
anent this muddy toiletbowl,
while kindred intellects evoke
allegiance per blunt instruments—
Olaf(being to all intents

(continued)

a corpse and wanting any rag
upon what God unto him gave)
responds, without getting annoyed
"I will not kiss your f.ing flag"

straightway the silver bird looked grave
(departing hurriedly to shave)

but—though all kinds of officers
(a yearning nation's blueeyed pride)
their passive prey did kick and curse
until for wear their clarion
voices and boots were much the worse,
and egged the firstclassprivates on
his rectum wickedly to tease
by means of skillfully applied

bayonets roasted hot with heat—
Olaf(upon what were once knees)
does almost ceaselessly repeat
"there is some s. I will not eat"

our president,being of which
assertions duly notified
threw the yellowsonofabitch
into a dungeon, where he died

Christ(of His mercy infinite)
i pray to see;and Olaf, too

preponderatingly because
unless statistics lie he was
more brave than me:more blond than you.

From *W[ViVa]*

MIXED REVIEWS

Cummings published his first book of poetry, *Tulips and Chimneys*, in 1923. Containing a variety of his experimental verses, the book got mixed reviews. Though some critics were confused and put off by what they perceived as Cummings's eccentric style, others appreciated his attempts to infuse poetry with the modernist spirit. "It is extraordinarily good," wrote one reviewer. "It contains, in its own individual and unprecedented style, as beautiful poems as have been written by any present-day poet in the English language."

Besides challenging the critics, Cummings upset several printers who were reluctant to reproduce his poems as written. Because of the peculiar spacing, punctuation, capitalization, and syntax that appeared in Cummings's work, some printers made "corrections" when they set the type, re-establishing what they saw as proper grammar and structure. This infuriated Cummings. He finally solved the problem by finding one printer—S. A. Jacobs—who understood what he was trying to do artistically. Together, Cummings and Jacobs oversaw the production of more than a dozen poetry books and prose collections that the poet published between 1925 and 1960.

noise no 13, *an oil painting by E. E. Cummings, 1925*

Buffalo Bill 's
defunct
        who used to
        ride a watersmooth-silver
                            stallion
and break onetwothreefourfive pigeonsjustlikethat
                                    Jesus

he was a handsome man
                    and what i want to know is
how do you like your blueeyed boy
Mister Death

From *Tulips and Chimneys*

One of the saddest periods in Cummings's life occurred shortly after his discharge from the army. He fell in love with Elaine Thayer, the wife of a close friend. The Thayers lived in separate residences, and Scofield Thayer was openly disdainful of conventional marriage. He actually encouraged Cummings to become involved with Elaine.

Cummings and Elaine had a daughter, Nancy, in 1919, but though the Thayers divorced when Nancy was a year old, Cummings continued to play the role of Elaine's boyfriend; he was perhaps unable to accept the roles of husband and father. He moved to Paris for two years, writing and painting by day and carousing with friends by night.

Before Nancy turned five, Elaine finally convinced Cummings to marry her, and he legally adopted Nancy a month later, in April 1924. When Elaine's sister unexpectedly died soon after the wedding, Cummings was less than supportive as his new wife struggled to make funeral arrangements and settle her sister's estate in Europe. Elaine took Nancy with her. On the outbound ship, she fell in love with a wealthy Irishman.

When Elaine asked him for a divorce, the shock jolted Cummings back to reality. He realized his behavior had driven his wife and child away. But Elaine would not change her mind, and after months of tortured negotiations, she got her divorce. She remarried and moved with her new husband to Ireland, taking Nancy with her.

Nancy grew up believing Scofield Thayer was her father. It wasn't until she was in her mid-20s that she learned the truth and made contact with Cummings. Though happy to see her, Cummings denied Nancy the close relationship she wanted. He preferred to love her as he had for most of her life—from a distance.

Cummings's first wife, Elaine Orr Thayer

it really must
be Nice, never to

have no imagination)or never
never to wonder about guys you used to(and them
slim hot queens with dam next to nothing

on)tangoing
(while a feller tries
to hold down the fifty bucks per
job with one foot and rock a

cradle with the other)it Must be
nice never to have no doubts about why you
put the ring
on(and watching her
face grow old and tired to which

you're married and hands get red washing
things and dishes)and to never, never really wonder i
mean about the smell
of babies and how you

know the dam rent's going to and everything and
never, never
Never to stand at no window
because i can't sleep(smoking sawdust

cigarettes in the
middle of the night

From *is 5*

27

In 1926, Cummings's parents were involved in an accident while on the way to Joy Farm. Driving in a snowstorm at night, Edward Cummings failed to stop at a railroad crossing, and his car was rammed by an oncoming train. He died instantly. Rebecca Cummings survived, thanks in part to the bedside support she received from her two children.

Though Cummings and his father had often been at odds over the years, there was a genuine bond of love between them. Before his death, Edward Cummings had made peace with his son, and the two men had established a warm friendship. But it wasn't until 13 years after Edward's death that Cummings was able to adequately and eloquently express his love for his father in the poem "my father moved through dooms of love." Writing that poem, Cummings later remarked, was the beginning for him of a new sense of moral responsibility as a poet.

Joy Farm, Silver Lake, N.H.

my father moved through dooms of love
through sames of am through haves of give,
singing each morning out of each night
my father moved through depths of height

this motionless forgetful where
turned at his glance to shining here;
that if(so timid air is firm)
under his eyes would stir and squirm

newly as from unburied which
floats the first who,his april touch
drove sleeping selves to swarm their fates
woke dreamers to their ghostly roots

and should some why completely weep
my father's fingers brought her sleep:
vainly no smallest voice might cry
for he could feel the mountains grow.

Lifting the valleys of the sea
my father moved through griefs of joy;
praising a forehead called the moon
singing desire into begin

joy was his song and joy so pure
a heart of star by him could steer
and pure so now and now so yes
the wrists of twilight would rejoice

keen as midsummer's keen beyond
conceiving mind of sun will stand,
so strictly(over utmost him
so hugely)stood my father's dream

his flesh was flesh his blood was blood:
no hungry man but wished him food;
no cripple wouldn't creep one mile
uphill to only see him smile.

(continued)

Scorning the pomp of must and shall
my father moved through dooms of feel;
his anger was as right as rain
his pity was as green as grain

septembering arms of year extend
less humbly wealth to foe and friend
than he to foolish and to wise
offered immeasurable is

proudly and(by octobering flame
beckoned)as earth will downward climb,
so naked for immortal work
his shoulders marched against the dark

his sorrow was as true as bread:
no liar looked him in the head;
if every friend became his foe
he'd laugh and build a world with snow.

My father moved through theys of we,
singing each new leaf out of each tree

(and every child was sure that spring
danced when she heard my father sing)

then let men kill which cannot share,
let blood and flesh be mud and mire,
scheming imagine,passion willed,
freedom a drug that's bought and sold

giving to steal and cruel kind,
a heart to fear,to doubt a mind,
to differ a disease of same,
conform the pinnacle of am

though dull were all we taste as bright,
bitter all utterly things sweet,
maggoty minus and dumb death
all we inherit,all bequeath

and nothing quite so least as truth
—i say though hate were why men breathe—
because my father lived his soul
love is the whole and more than all

From 50 Poems

LOVE

Following his short-lived marriage to Elaine, Cummings became involved in a seven-year relationship with a vivacious woman named Anne Barton. When Cummings married Anne in 1929, his mother gave him Joy Farm as a wedding present. But Anne's inability to be faithful, as well as his inability to make enough money to support the free-spending lifestyle she loved, ultimately led to their divorce in 1932. She immediately married a wealthy surgeon.

Soon after his divorce from Anne, Cummings met and fell in love with Marion Morehouse, an elegant and stunningly beautiful model and actress. Her sophistication, combined with an appreciation for simple things—walks in the park, dinner in small Italian restaurants, fresh flowers—made her alluring to Cummings. And her organizational and business skills made her indispensable to him professionally. Though they never formally married, Cummings introduced Marion as his wife for the rest of his life.

Anne Barton, 1927

somewhere i have never travelled,gladly beyond
any experience,your eyes have their silence:
in your most frail gesture are things which enclose me,
or which i cannot touch because they are too near

your slightest look easily will unclose me
though i have closed myself as fingers,
you open always petal by petal myself as Spring opens
(touching skillfully,mysteriously)her first rose

or if your wish be to close me,i and
my life will shut very beautifully,suddenly,
as when the heart of this flower imagines
the snow carefully everywhere descending;

(continued)

nothing which we are to perceive in this world equals
the power of your intense fragility:whose texture
compels me with the colour of its countries,
rendering death and forever with each breathing

(i do not know what it is about you that closes
and opens;only something in me understands
the voice of your eyes is deeper than all roses)
nobody,not even the rain,has such small hands

From *W[ViVa]*

THE ARTIST

By the time he was in his 30s, Cummings had become an accomplished, though not particularly distinctive, visual artist. He had shown his abstract paintings in a few large New York exhibitions, done commissioned works for friends and family members, and occasionally contributed ink drawings to magazines.

Gradually, Cummings's infatuation with abstract art gave way to an interest in realism. The result was the 1931 publication of *CIOPW*, a book filled with drawings and paintings of people and places. (The title stood for charcoal, ink, oil, pencil, and watercolor.) Later that same year, he mounted a one-man exhibit of similar works in a New York gallery. A *New York Times* critic remarked, "Cummings the painter, like Cummings the poet, is first of all an intelligent experimenter."

Although his work as a visual artist never earned him the same recognition and appreciation as his poetry, Cummings continued to draw and paint throughout the rest of his life.

"View From My Room," a pencil drawing by Cummings depicting the scene outside a Paris hotel

Picasso

you give us Things

which

bulge:grunting lungs pumped full of sharp thick mind

you make us shrill

presents always

shut in the sumptuous screech of

simplicity

(out of the

black unbunged

Something gushes vaguely a squeak of planes

or

between squeals of

Nothing grabbed with circular shrieking tightness

solid screams whisper.)

Lumberman of The Distinct

your brain's

axe only chops hugest inherent

Trees of Ego,from

whose living and biggest

bodies lopped

of every

prettiness

you hew form truly

From *XLI Poems*

POLITICAL CHANGE

As a young man, Cummings had supported left-wing politics and pacifism, but as he grew older he became increasingly conservative. His political transformation began in 1931 when he toured the Soviet Union. There he found a political system that he felt stifled individual expression and repressed individual rights. For Cummings, this was intolerable. "I loathed it," he later said of Soviet communism.

Eventually, Cummings came to detest not only communism but any political philosophy that he perceived as compromising individual rights for the benefit of the state. He became bitterly opposed to liberal American politics, which cost him some of his friends in New York literary and art circles.

However, Cummings did retain his outlook on pacifism throughout his life. Many of his most satirical poems deal with his opposition to war, the blind patriotism he believed to be the cause, and the wastefulness of lives that results from armed conflict.

Moscow's Red Square, 1932: Troops and workers celebrate the 15th anniversary of the Bolshevik Revolution

when serpents bargain for the right to squirm
and the sun strikes to gain a living wage—
when thorns regard their roses with alarm
and rainbows are insured against old age

when every thrush may sing no new moon in
if all screech-owls have not okayed his voice
—and any wave signs on the dotted line
or else an ocean is compelled to close

when the oak begs permission of the birch
to make an acorn—valleys accuse their
mountains of having altitude—and march
denounces april as a saboteur

then we'll believe in that incredible
unanimal mankind(and not until)

From *XAIPE*

In 1947, Cummings's mother died at the age of 87 after suffering a stroke. At her funeral, Cummings's sister Elizabeth read a poem he'd written for their mother several years earlier, entitled "if there are any heavens."

The loss of his mother was both an emotional and a financial blow to Cummings. For years, Rebecca Cummings had subsidized her son's unorthodox lifestyle by sending him a monthly allowance. Now living expenses and the upkeep of both his New York apartment and Joy Farm quickly used up the money he'd inherited from his mother's estate.

In need of a new source of income, Cummings began touring the country giving poetry readings. These tours, in addition to paying well, gave him a chance to introduce his poetry to a variety of audiences, which improved sales of his books. He quickly established a reputation as one of America's finest public readers.

At the height of his popularity as a reader, Cummings was in his early 60s. By then, he hated the rigorous travel schedules his tours demanded, but he loved the attention he attracted. Seated behind a table, Cummings alternated reading prose passages and poems, skillfully revealing the beauty and humor in his works.

After attending a Cummings reading in Boston in 1957, a reviewer for *Harper's* magazine wrote: "The big crowd loved him. He read slowly, meaningfully, lovingly—lingering on each syllable without losing for an instant the drive and surge of his poems…. Though it is banal to say over and over that poetry is something to be heard, one must say it—and say it again—to describe Cummings's impact on his listeners."

Cummings at his New York City apartment

if there are any heavens my mother will(all
        by herself) have
one. It will not be a pansy heaven nor
a fragile heaven of lilies-of-the-valley but
it will be a heaven of blackred roses

my father will be(deep like a rose
tall like a rose)

standing near my

(swaying over her
silent)
with eyes which are really petals and see

nothing with the face of a poet really which
is a flower and not a face with
hands
which whisper
This is my beloved my

        (suddenly in sunlight
he will bow,

& the whole garden will bow)

From W[ViVa]

FINAL READING

Cummings spent the afternoon of September 2, 1962, splitting firewood in the barn on Joy Farm, as he'd done so often since boyhood. When he finished, he went back to the house to clean up for dinner. On his way upstairs, he collapsed. Marion telephoned for help, but there was nothing anyone could do. Cummings had had a brain hemorrhage. At 1:15 A.M. on September 3, he died at the age of 67. A few days later, in a small private ceremony, the poet was buried in a Boston cemetery, not far from the graves of his father and mother.

Ten years earlier, Cummings had introduced the last lecture in a series with these lines, which in retrospect seemed to sum up his life:

"Ecstasy and anguish, being and becoming; the immortality of the creative imagination and the indomitability of the human spirit—these are the subjects of my final poetry reading."

E. E. Cummings, 1894–1962

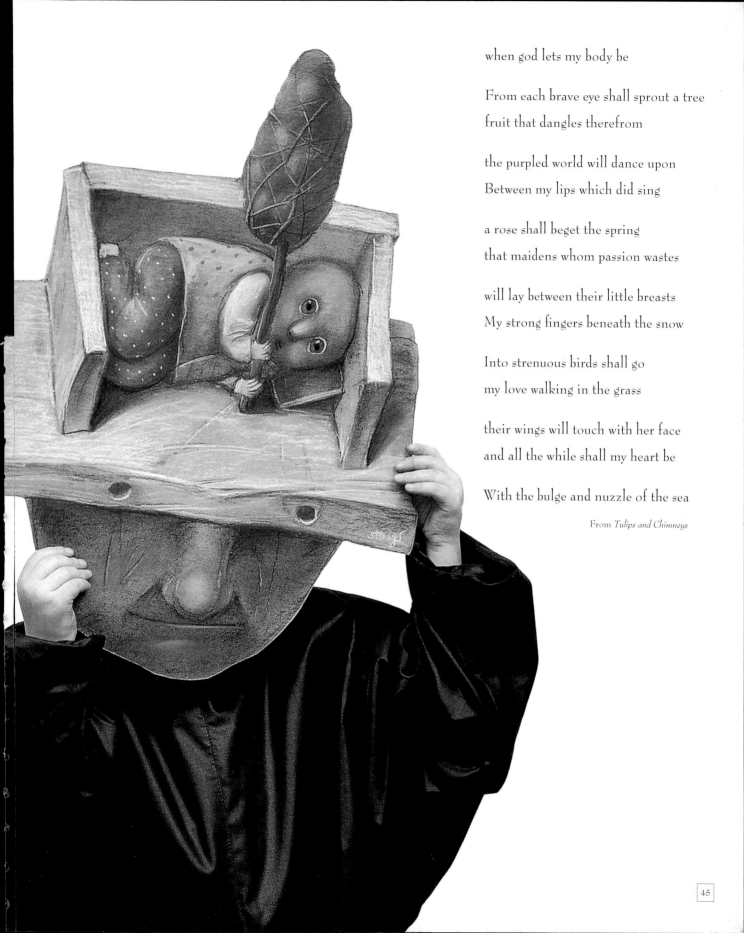

when god lets my body be

From each brave eye shall sprout a tree
fruit that dangles therefrom

the purpled world will dance upon
Between my lips which did sing

a rose shall beget the spring
that maidens whom passion wastes

will lay between their little breasts
My strong fingers beneath the snow

Into strenuous birds shall go
my love walking in the grass

their wings will touch with her face
and all the while shall my heart be

With the bulge and nuzzle of the sea

From *Tulips and Chimneys*

ACKNOWLEDGMENTS

PHOTO CREDITS

Nancy T. Andrews; Cambridge Historical Commission; The Everett Collection; The Granger Collection; The Houghton Library, Harvard College Library; Library of Congress Prints & Photographs Division [LC-USZ62-106232]; Marion Morehouse; Photo Researchers, Inc.

POETRY CREDITS

SELECTED WORKS BY E. E. CUMMINGS

POETRY

Tulips and Chimneys, 1923

XLI Poems, 1925

is 5, 1926

W[ViVa], 1931

No thanks, 1935

Collected Poems, 1938

50 Poems, 1940

1 x 1 [One Times One], 1944

XAIPE: 71 Poems, 1950

Poems 1923–1954, 1954

95 Poems, 1958

100 Selected Poems, 1959

73 Poems, 1963

Complete Poems 1923–1962, 1972

Complete Poems 1904–1962, 1991

PROSE

The Enormous Room, 1922

Eimi [I Am], 1933

i: six nonlectures, 1953

Fairy Tales, 1965

OTHER WORKS

Him (play), 1927

CIOPW (artwork), 1931

INDEX

Poems appearing in this work (by first line):

all ignorance toboggans into know 13

Buffalo Bill's 25

the Cambridge ladies who live in furnished souls 16

I lift my eyes. 18

i sing of Olaf glad and big 21–22

if there are any heavens my mother will(all by herself)have 43

in Just- 10

it really must 27

l(a 7

my father moved through dooms of love 31–32

Picasso 38

somewhere i have never travelled,glady beyond 35–36

when god lets my body be 45

when serpents bargain for the right to squirm 41

you shall above all things be glad and young. 1

Brown, Slater 17

Cambridge Latin School (Mass.) 12, 14

Cambridge Review 12

CIOPW 37

communism 40

Cubism 15

Cummings, Anne Barton (second wife) 34

Cummings, Edward (father) 5, 8, 15, 17, 29, 44

Cummings, Edward Estlin (E. E.)
books and writings 5, 6, 24, 42
childhood 8
critical appraisal 24, 37, 42
death 44
education 12, 14
employment 17
favorite books 12
marriages and partnerships 26, 34
military service 17, 20
move to New York City 17, 20
pacifism 17, 40
as painter and visual artist 15, 37
poetic form and technique 5, 6, 20, 24
poetic themes 5, 6, 40
poetry readings 42, 44
and political philosophy 40
social life 14–15, 26
values, artistic and personal 15, 20

Cummings, Elaine Thayer (first wife) 26, 34

Cummings, Elizabeth (sister) 8, 42

Cummings, Rebecca (mother) 8, 14, 29, 34, 42, 44

The Enormous Room (autobiography) 17

Harper's 42

Harvard University 5, 8, 12, 14, 15

"if there are any heavens" 42

is Five 6

Jacobs, S. A. 24

Joy Farm (N.H.) 8, 20, 29, 34, 42, 44

Morehouse, Marion (partner) 34, 44

"my father moved through dooms of love" 5, 29

New York Times 37

Norton-Harjes Ambulance Corps 17

Soviet Union 40

Thayer, Nancy (daughter) 26

Thayer, Scofield 26

Tulips and Chimneys 24

World War I 17

Published by Creative Education
P.O. Box 227, Mankato, Minnesota 56002
Creative Education is an imprint of The Creative Company
www.thecreativecompany.us
Design by Stephanie Blumenthal
Production by The Design Lab
Artwork by Stasys Eidrigevicius
Art direction by Rita Marshall
Printed in the United States of America
Copyright © 2015 Creative Education
Library of Congress Cataloging-in-Publication Data
Berry, S. L.
E. E. Cummings / by S. L. Berry.
p. cm. — (Voices in Poetry)
Includes index.
Summary: An exploration of the life and work of 20th-century American writer
E. E. Cummings, whose poetry is known for its combination of innovative,
artistic style and traditional rhyme and meter.
ISBN 978-1-60818-325-8
1. Cummings, E. E. (Edward Estlin), 1894–1962—Juvenile literature. 2.
Poets, American—20th century—Biography—Juvenile literature. 3. Young
adult poetry, American. I. Title.
PS3505.U334Z563 2014
811'.52—dc23   [B]   2013030155

CCSS: RL.4.1, 2, 3, 4, 5, 6; RL.5.2, 4, 6, 7; RI.5.1, 2, 3, 8
First Edition
9 8 7 6 5 4 3 2 1